AF333388

A TRIBUTE

To Our Parents And The Entire WWII Generation

From The Baby Boomers, For All You've Accomplished

Christopher Publishing

Newport Beach, California

Published by:
Christopher Publishing
P.O. Box #333
Newport Beach, CA 92625

Printed in the United States of America

ISBN 0-9662871-2-6

Publisher's Cataloging-in-Publication

White, Chris, 1956-
  A tribute to our parents and the entire WWII generation
from the baby boomers, for all you have accomplished /
[Chris White] – 1st ed. p. cm.

    1.   World War, 1939-1945—Social aspects—United States. 2.
Baby boom generation—Family relationships. 3. United States
—social life and customs—1918-1945. I. Title.

D744.7U6W45 1998   973.91
                          QBI98-119

Library of Congress Catalog Number 98-92402

Dedication

To my parents Dean and Barbara White, who were the inspiration for this book. They started their journey together after World War II while living in the basement of my grandparents' home in Shelby, Indiana—a town of one hundred people. My father, a merchant marine veteran, is mostly known for his success building an empire of billboards and hotels across America; but quite honestly he was an even better father...one who was always there. My mother was very representative of the women from the World War II generation, whose priorities were the needs of others, well before their own. Myself, my brothers Bruce and Craig, and my sister Cindy agree: it would have been difficult for our parents to have been better ones.

Table of Contents

(optional)

Memorable

Family

Photo(s)

A Personal Tribute to:

____

From: _______________________________

____

Date:

Acknowledgements

Thanks to Richard Martini and all of my other friends for their feedback and encouragement along the way. You have no idea what it meant to me.

Also, a heartfelt thanks to Janice Phelps, of BookWorld Press, for professionalism of the highest caliber, and Rosie Grupp, for true passion, hard work, and skillful design of the book.

*I*ntroduction

As the baby boomer generation completes receiving the torch being passed on to them by their parents, the boomers eagerly anticipate what they will do with America during their "watch." But first we should take a moment to look back one more time at what might be the greatest generation in American history—the World War II generation. This generation's sacrifices and leadership made America what it is today. Unquestionably, this generation had its problems and imperfections, but accomplishments far outweigh failures. For all their great sacrifices and achievements, we baby boomers owe these people a thank you that may not have been properly bestowed—which is the inspiration for *A Tribute to Our Parents and the Entire WWII Generation.*

To every individual from the WWII generation who reads this book—please enjoy this tribute to you—from myself and all of the other baby boomer children. You deserve it! This book is not just for the generation being honored inside its pages, but also for their future descendants who can look back, and keep the memory alive of this special generation who meant so much in American history.

—*Christopher Dean White*

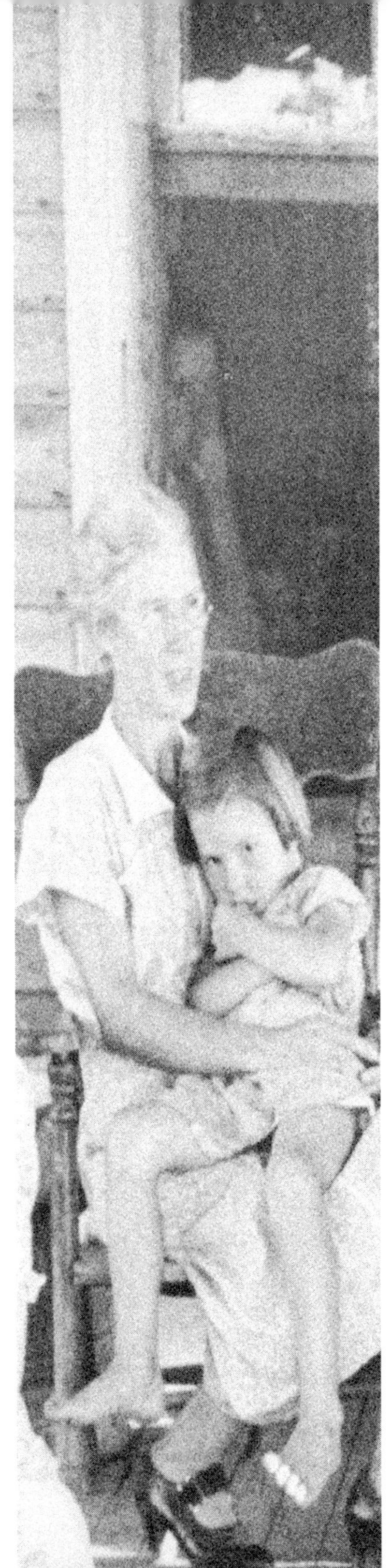

Depression

There may be no better way to understand why the people of the World War II (WWII) generation prevailed through continuous critical challenges than to remember that they grew up during the most difficult economic era in our nation's history—the Great Depression of 1929 to 1940.

A family is forced to live in a tent during the depression.

This socio-economic catastrophe affected virtually everyone, and for a long period of time. Many members of the WWII generation, including some of the wealthiest families in America, saw their parents lose everything and face the challenge of rebuilding their lives.

It is estimated that during the early 1930s between twelve and fifteen million people were out of work—a 25 percent unemployment rate! As the Dow Jones average crashed from 300 to 70, farm prices lost up to 90 percent of their pre–stock market crash (1929) prices. The economic panic caused approximately one fourth of all banks to fail. Retail sales fell 50 percent after the crash and didn't rebound until 1937. Approximately one thousand people lost their homes to

A breadline in New York City in 1929.

...in danger of total collapse.

foreclosure every day—eventually totalling millions of Americans. No one knew how to stop the panic, and the democratic structure was never more in danger of total collapse. The Hoover administration kept insisting things would get better if the government adopted a hands-off approach and refrained from involvement in economic aid. They encouraged the fortunate few with jobs to help those in soup lines. Most people helped as much as they could.

It wasn't until the Roosevelt administration was elected in 1932 and instituted the "New Deal" that things got better. Roosevelt renewed consumer confidence and passed the Glass-Steagall Act that formed the Federal Deposit Insurance Corporation (FDIC); he even established a bank holiday. The FDIC insured deposits at member banks for up to $5,000 and forbade banks from dealing in stocks and bonds.

In addition, less than one hundred days after taking office, the new administration had already created the "alphabet agencies"—an amazing feat. Many of the WWII generation worked as young men for the Civilian Conservation Corps (CCC). By end of the summer in 1933, approximately 300,000 young people were working in the CCC camps, and by the time it was dismantled, over two and a half million youths had participated. It was estimated that they had planted over 200 million trees; they also did valuable work to reduce floods and built many campgrounds still in existence today. Later the Civil Works Administration (CWA) was formed.

...finally put an end to the crisis.

This agency employed over four million people and concentrated on restoring urban areas. The Workers Progress Administration (WPA) performed infra-structure improvements to highways, buildings, and so forth. When the WPA was disbanded in 1943, it had employed approximately fifteen million Americans and had helped them make it through this crisis period. The Agricultural Adjustment Act (AAA) was also an important part of the New Deal. The AAA paid farmers a subsidy to reduce crop production and alleviate the crop surplus problem. Later an Emergency Farm Mortgage Act was passed to protect farmers from foreclosures.

President Roosevelt's New Deal, and all the agencies he formed, put America back to work. It was not enough to totally overcome the Depression; however, it was good enough to stabilize things until the large pre-WWII industrial build-up finally put an end to the crisis. Most Americans, those who weren't alive during the Great Depression, can't imagine such an ordeal. The fact that the World War II generation came of age during this desperate time in American history explains much of the tremendous resiliency for which they are known.

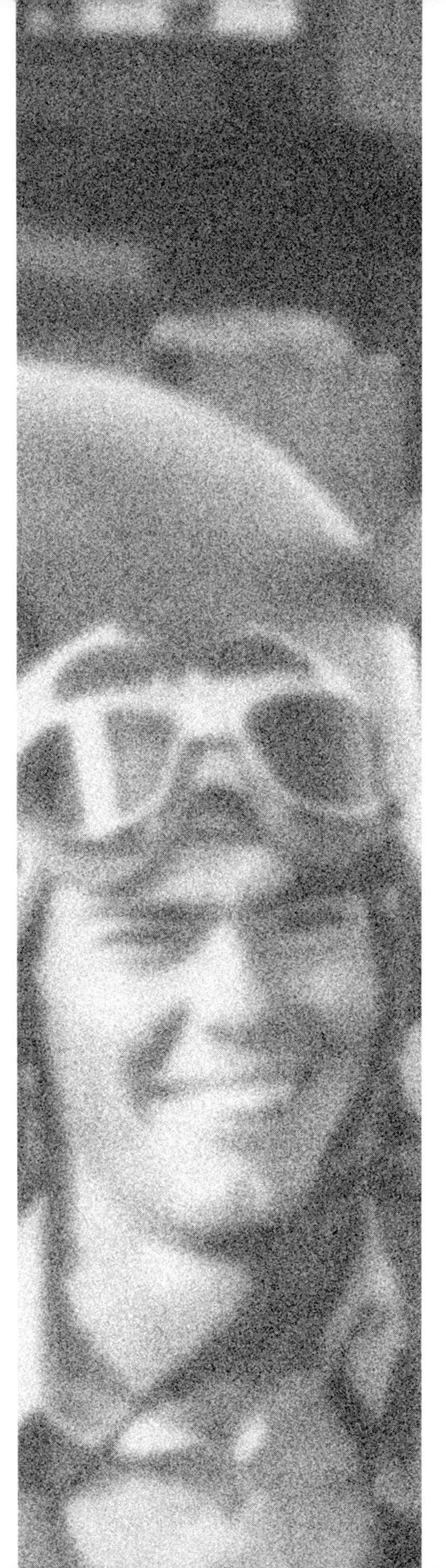

World War II
and Korea

Almost exactly ten years after the stock market crash of 1929, Poland, Britain, and France declared war on Germany. Although President Franklin D. Roosevelt declared the United States a neutral nation, most people knew the neutrality probably wouldn't last. When Hitler and Mussolini (the Axis) agreed to fight against Britain and France, America soon found itself involved as an Allied power. Meanwhile (as if there wasn't enough trouble in Europe), relations between the US and Japan (an Axis power) were in

"USS Shaw" exploding during the Japanese raid on "Pearl Harbor," December 7, 1941.

serious trouble because America demanded withdrawal of all Japanese troops from China. On December 7, 1941, Japanese planes bombarded the American base at Pearl Harbor, Hawaii, sinking or damaging six battleships and about one hundred fifty airplanes, killing 2,400 people. The next day, President Roosevelt declared war on Japan—in response, Germany and Italy immediately declared war on the United States. The world was at war. Five days before Christmas in 1941, Roosevelt signed the Draft Act, which called for all men between the ages of 18 and 65 to register for the military; men between 20 and 44 were considered "active."

The famous WWII war effort commenced as all Americans cooperated in any way they could to support the American fighters. This included rationing of rubber (which meant shoes), butter, sugar, gasoline, and many other items. People at home loyally replaced those who were overseas serving their country, even those on the farms. By the middle of the war, over two million women were part of the home-front replacements. Many women worked building warships as welders, assemblers, mechanics, and so forth.

...the Allies turned things around...

The USO volunteer organization was also formed so service personnel could have a place to meet their personal and social needs while off duty. Citizens purchased approximately 150 billion dollars of war stamps and bonds to support the effort. Many new taxes were levied with little complaint. By the end of the war, the effort at home was responsible for building almost 15,000 ships, 300,000 airplanes, 85,000 tanks, and an enormous number of vehicles and quantities of ammunition.

Six months after the United States joined the war, the situation did not look promising for the Allies. The Germans controlled most of Europe and the most forbidding part of Africa; they were also tearing through Russia. Meanwhile, the Japanese—a world power by themselves—controlled most of Southeast Asia and the Pacific Rim. Even Australia, New Zealand, and India would have had reason to fear conquest if things had continued in the same way, but somehow the Allies turned things around about halfway through 1942 when the Americans won the Battle of Midway by destroying four Japanese aircraft carriers. Then, in 1943, General Eisenhower invaded Sicily by way of sea and went on to capture the rest of Italy. But an invasion of Central Europe was considered necessary if the Germans were to be finally defeated.

MARINES SALUTE
COAST GUARD
FOR THEIR BIG PART IN
THE INVASION OF
GUAM
"THEY PUT US HERE AND
WE INTEND TO STAY"

The U.S. Marines salute the U.S. Coast Guard after the fury of battle had subsided and the Japanese on Guam had been defeated.

1944 color poster by Steele Salvage

…another atomic bomb was dropped…

On June 6, 1944, the Allied troops landed on the coast of Normandy, France, on what would become known as D-Day. Approximately 175,000 Allied troops invaded Germany that day, and nearly one thousand brave American soldiers died at Omaha beach alone. In all, roughly one million American soldiers had entered France. By September 1944, the Allies took Paris and had liberated most of the countries the Germans had seized. In March of 1945, the Germans retreated across the Rhine River towards Berlin. On May 8, Germany finally surrendered and the war in Europe was over.

Meanwhile, in the Pacific, Americans were also succeeding, capturing most of the small islands. After a lengthy battle of about eight months, they finally won in the Philippines, but suffered heavy casualties. The invasion and conquest of Japan would be necessary to end the war completely. President Harry S. Truman warned the Japanese that if they didn't surrender, they would face tremendous casualties. The Japanese refused to surrender and an atomic bomb was dropped on the Japanese city of Hiroshima. When no sign of surrender was forthcoming, another atomic bomb was dropped on the city of Nagasaki. About a week later, Japan finally surrendered and WWII was over at last.

Many of the WWII generation who survived the war wouldn't have lived past 1945 if a mass military invasion of Japan had occurred. Unfortunately, over 400,000 courageous Americans did die in WWII, fighting to save the world from the tyranny it faced. The contributions of those who faced combat and those that participated in the invaluable war effort will not be forgotten.

THE *Korean war*

Not long after America found itself appreciating the peace that followed World War II, another world problem developed that could not be ignored. Toward the end of the 1940s, after Mao Tse-Tung prevailed in the Chinese Civil War, Communism was making significant advances in Asia. In June of 1950, the Communist North Korean Army crossed the thirty-eighth parallel to attack the Republic of South Korea. President Truman had no choice but to commit American troops to the United Nations effort to defeat North Korea in this aggressive action. The United Nations organized an army comprised of

Men work their way over the snowy mountains about 10 miles north of Seoul, Korea, attempting to locate the enemy lines and positions.

forces from sixteen different countries; the intent was to push the North Koreans back to the proper side of the thirty-eighth parallel. Approximately 90 percent of the United Nations troops were either American or South Korean. This was a major conflict. America, just starting anew after WWII, found itself at war again.

In November of 1950, the Chinese became directly involved in the Korean conflict when some of their troops joined the North Koreans. As the American government considered the possibility of war with China, they faced the unthinkable ramification of this action—World War III! President Truman decided that military intervention with the Chinese wasn't necessary. The Korean War remained in stalemate for approximately two more years.

Then in July 1953 an agreement was reached, and the boundaries remained the same as before the war started. Unfortunately, an estimated thirty-four thousand American lives were lost. By the end of the war, about three million Americans had seen combat. Coming on the heels of WWII, and being small in comparison, the Korean War is often known as the "forgotten war." It is important for future generations not to forget the sacrifices made by those WWII generation members who rose to the occasion yet once again in Korea, and how this important conflict almost became World War III!

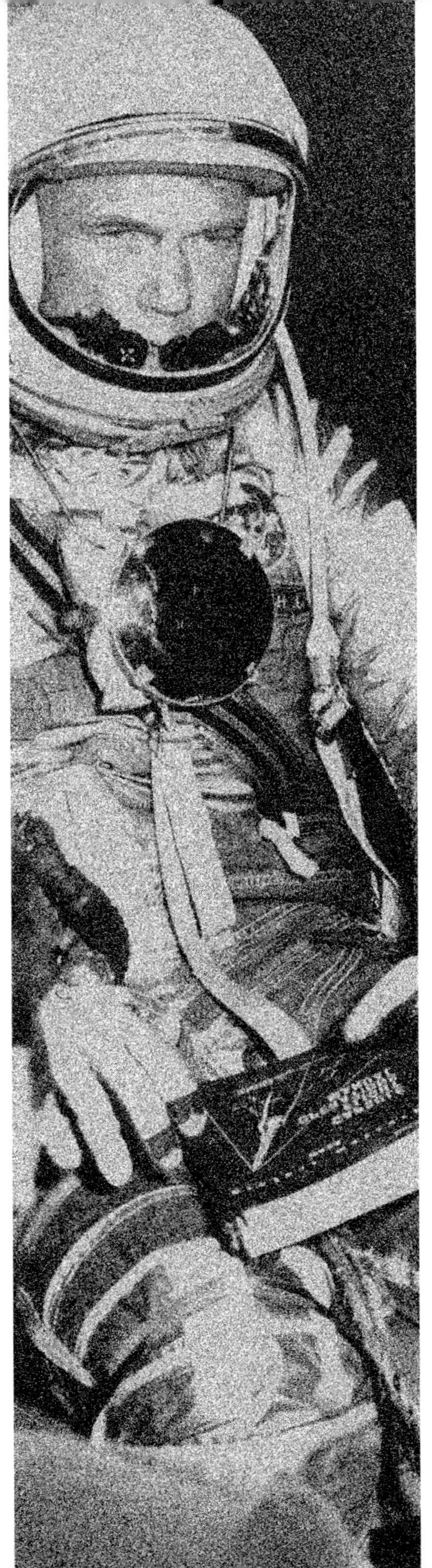

WINNING THE Space race

In October of 1957, the Soviet Union successfully launched a satellite into orbit. The United States anticipated a terrible defeat as it looked like its Cold War rival was far ahead in what many considered a field vital to the future. Approximately three months later, the United States successfully launched a satellite into orbit.

Both the United States and the Soviet Union had been experimenting with human test pilots flying at supersonic speeds. This was considered a prerequisite to a manual space flight. In 1947 Chuck Yaeger (b 1923) broke the sound barrier. In 1959 the nation's first seven astronauts were selected. After being elected president in 1960, John F. Kennedy (b 1917) declared that putting a man on the moon within the next decade was a primary concern. However, the Soviet Union found itself well in the lead again— in April of 1961, they put an astronaut into outer space.

*Cape Canaveral,
Florida— Astronaut
John Glenn is suited
up in preparation for
a simulated test,
January 21, 1962.*

The United States still had hopes of winning this contest. In May, Alan B. Shepard (b 1923) was the first American to explore space. In February of 1962, astronaut John Glenn (b 1921) orbited the earth three times. This was followed by Astronaut Scott Carpenter (b 1925) orbiting three times in May of 1962, and then Wally Schirra (b 1923) orbiting six times. In May of 1963, Major L. Gordon Cooper (b 1927) orbited twenty-two times.

The Gemini program was started to analyze the effects of long-term flights on astronauts. In 1966 the Apollo program was launched. This was the final phase toward reaching the then late-President Kennedy's goal of putting a man on the moon. Meanwhile, the Russians had a tremendous setback when one of their missions ended in disaster and an astronaut died. Unfortunately, the United States suffered a major tragedy of its own in January of 1967 when astronauts Virgil "Gus" Grissom (b 1926), Roger Chafee (b 1935), and Edward White (b 1930) died while conducting tests on the launch pad.

Merritt Island Launch Area, Florida,—Gemini VII Astronaut Frank Borman, Command Pilot for the National Aeronautics and Space Administration's planned 14 day orbital mission, has his space suit checked by suit technician during weight and balance tests. Nov. 8, 1965.

Manned Spacecraft Center, Houston, Texas— Apollo Prime Crew— The National Aeronautics and Space Administration has named these astronauts as the prime crew of the first manned Apollo space flight. Left to right are Edward H. White II, Virgil I. Grissom, and Roger B. Chaffee. April 1, 1966.

*...making
the space
program a top
priority and
declaring the
dream.*

This terrible accident didn't stop NASA from continuing toward its goal. Apollo flights from Wally Schirra (b 1923), Donn Eisele (b 1930), Frank Borman (b 1928), James Lovell Jr. (b 1928), James A. McDivitt (b 1929), Thomas P. Stafford (b 1930), and John W. Young (b 1930) made NASA conclude it was ready to attempt the "dream." On July 21, 1969, Apollo 11 astronauts Neil Armstrong, (b 1930), Buzz Aldrin (b 1930), and Michael Collins (b 1930) fulfilled the dream. Not only was it a significant victory in the Cold War, but as Neil Armstrong said, "A giant leap for mankind."

By early 1969, the United States led Russia by a wide margin in the space race. The United States led in manual flights, 19 to 12; space links, 9 to 0; space walks, 10 to 3; and moon orbits, 1 to 0.

The American space program has continued to achieve unimaginable feats over the decades since that famous day in July of 1969. Like the rest of the world, the Russians could only look on in amazement. Their space program continued to fall very far behind. Given the United States' position behind the Russians in the early 1960s, it was astonishing not only that the Americans prevailed, but that they did so in such a big way. President John F. Kennedy, the first president of the WWII generation, deserves a tremendous amount of credit for making the space program a top priority and declaring the dream.

Obviously all of the pilots and NASA personnel responsible for winning the space race deserve credit also. These people created the model for NASA—a program that has remained one of the most respected organizations anywhere. Neil Armstrong setting his foot on the moon in July of 1969 will undoubtedly remain one of this generation's greatest moments.

Science, medicine & technology

Just as spectacular as any of the other accomplishments of the WWII generation is their contribution to the advancement of science, medicine, and technology. How did America emerge so quickly from a time in the 1950s when there was little hope against many ills and diseases, to a time in 1990 where open-heart surgeries were commonplace and the average life expectancy was approximately seventy-five years. How did America evolve from the development of first general-purpose digital computer in 1944 with its numerous problems, to the incredible applications of computers today? The answer lies in the decision of the WWII generation to invest as much as possible in research, development, and education, and in their determination to succeed. Obviously it is not possible to list all of the scientific, medical, and technological contributions for this generation, but a chronological list of the major advancements follows:

1944 The first automatic computer is completed at Harvard University by professor Howard Hathway Allen (b 1900).

1946 British transatlantic passenger air service to North America starts; the flying time is about twenty hours.

1946 The (ENIAC) Electronic Numeric Integration and Computer, the world's first automatic computer, is introduced by University of Pennsylvania engineers John Eckert (b 1919) and John Mauchly (b 1907).

1947 The *Spruce Goose* is built and flown by Howard Hughes (b 1905).

1947 Instant photography is invented by Polaroid company founder Edward Land (b 1907).

1948 Physicists Richard Phillips Feynman (b 1918) and Julian Schwinger (b 1918) develop the theory of electrodynamics.

1948   The development of the transistor is announced by physicists William Schockley (b 1910), John Bardeen (b 1908), and Walter Brittain (b 1902).

1949   The Parke/Davis Company introduces the antibiotic chloroampherical as the first major breakthrough against typhoid fever.

1951   The US Atomic Energy Commission builds its first power producing nuclear reactor.

1951   Remington Rand offers the Univac computer commercially.

1952   Microbiologist Jonas Salk (b 1914) tests a vaccine against polio, which is later announced as a cure.

1952   Chemist H. Herbert Fox (b 1915) develops Isoniazid, a drug that is found to be effective against tuberculosis.

1952   US genetic researcher James Watson (b 1928) reveals his DNA theory, which later is corroborated through other world experiments.

1953   Jay Forester (b 1918) finishes developing magnetic core memory storage, which replaces electrostatic tubes in computers.

1954   The *Nautilus*, America's first nuclear power submarine, is launched. It was built at the request of Rear Admiral George Rickover (b 1900).

1956   The first videotape recorder is shown at an Ampex Corporation laboratory. It was developed by Charles Ginsburg (b 1920) and was first used by CBS television.

1956   US Marine pilot John Glenn (b 1921) sets a new transcontinental speed record, flying coast to coast in only three hours and twenty minutes.

1958   The first US Satellite is launched.

1959   The microchip is invented by Jack Kilsey (b 1927) and Robert Noyce (b 1927). Noyce later founded the Intel Corporation, which invents the microprocessor that makes the personal computer possible.

1959 Librium is developed by Chemist Leo Sternbadi (b 1907).

1960 The first ruby laser is built by Theodore Maiman (b 1927).

1961 Elliot Fetee Noyes (b 1910) designs and introduces the IBM electric typewriter, which revolutionized typewriters.

1962 Houston, Texas surgeon Michael De Bakey (b 1908) does the first artificial heart surgery using a ventricle bypass pump to assist the heart.

1962 The Lear jet is introduced by William Lear (b 1902). Lear also developed the eight-track tape player for music.

1964 Lockheed Corporation announces it now has a model jet capable of 2000 miles per hour.

1965 The world's first commercial satellite is put into orbit.

1966 MIT biochemist Har Go Bind Khorana (b 1922) announces the deciphering of the genetic code.

1967 Dr. Andrew Kantrowitz (b 1918) performs America's first heart transplant.

1967 An L-dopa theory developed by Dr. George Cotzias (b 1918) is announced as a partial treatment for Parkinson's disease.

1967 Benjamin Rubin (b 1917) invents the bifurotul vaccination needle that saved many lives around the world from smallpox.

1969 Astronaut Neil Armstrong (b 1930) is the first man on the moon.

1970 Biologist Daniel Nathins (b 1929) discovers that the DNA in a tumor virus can be "broken up."

1971 Biochemist Andrew Schallwy (b 1927) isolates the hormone ZLTRLT, which is part of human ovulation.

1974 Cincinnati Doctor Henry Heimlich (b 1920) introduces the Heimlich maneuver for saving people who are choking on food.

Dr. Robert Maurer

C. Everett Koop

1976 The FDA approves the use of Inderal to treat high blood pressure.

1978 Five new nuclear power plants open.

1980 The US Spacecraft *Voyager I* explores Saturn.

1981 Roger Sperry (b 1913) wins a Nobel prize for his discoveries in cerebral research.

1982 US Surgeon General C. Everett Koop (b 1917) calls cigarette smoking the chief preventable cause of death.

1983 Barbara McClintock (b 1902), a molecular biologist who made tremendous discoveries in genetic research, receives the Nobel prize in medicine.

1988 Gertrude Elion (b 1918) wins a Nobel prize in medicine for drug research.

1991 Alven Elrod (b 1928) receives a patent for a new electronic variable camshaft for automobiles.

1993 Robert Maurer (b 1924) is inducted into the Inventors Hall of Fame for his cooperative efforts in producing the first optical fiber, which revolutionized telecommunications.

1995 Dr. Jonas Salk (b 1926) dies while still working towards an AIDS cure.

*M*usic

Even though the generation that preceded the WWII generation made significant contributions to music, it wasn't until the "swing" music of WWII that American music received true world recognition. Swing music originated as a jazz style and was characterized by an ensemble (usually ten to fifteen instruments), playing various sections of big band music to rhythms ideal for dancing.

Glenn Miller

Benny Goodman (b 1909) was the first musician to make this musical style popular, and thus was named "the King of Swing." Others who followed were Tommy Dorsey (b 1905) and his brother Jimmy Dorsey (b 1904), Artie Shaw (b 1910), Glenn Miller (b 1904), Count Basie (b 1904), Les Brown (b 1912), and Duke Ellington (b 1899). It is widely believed Duke Ellington gave swing music its name. It was also known as "be-bop."

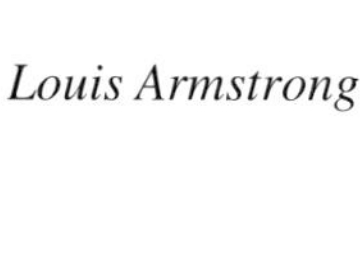

Louis Armstrong

Duke Ellington and his band.

...America's biggest contribution to world music.

American modern jazz, considered by many as America's biggest contribution to world music, also became quite popular during the 1940s. Charley "Bird" Parker (b 1920) and Dizzy Gillespie (b 1917) were the pioneers of this jazz movement. Trumpeter, bandleader, and composer Miles Davis (b 1926) followed his idol Charley Parker as one of the most famous and gifted performers in this musical genre. John Coltrane (b 1926), who toured with Davis, is known as one of the best sax players of all time. Dave Brubeck (b 1920) is credited with adding a new dimension to the "modern" or progressive jazz sound.

Also among the notable musicians from this era was trumpet player Louis "Satchmo" (an abbreviation of Satchelmouth) Armstrong (b 1900). Armstrong was a New Orleans native who not only played with other swing bands, but also had his own orchestra and was known for his gravely-toned voice and Dixieland jazz style. Armstrong is also credited with encouraging a young Lionel Hampton (b 1903) to take up the vibraphone, where Hampton flourished and became a legend in his own right.

The "Rat Pack". From left, Frank Sinatra, Dean Martin, Sammy Davis Jr., Peter Lawford and Joey Bishop.

Nat King Cole

The most popular singers from the WWII generation, who are all still very popular today and will always be American singing icons, were the members of the "Rat Pack." These singers included Frank Sinatra (b 1915), Dean Martin (b 1917), and Sammy Davis Jr. (b 1926). Another Italian-American male ballad singer like Sinatra whose popularity remains high today is Tony Bennett (b 1926). Others whose singing will remain a part of American musical history from the WWII generation are Ella Fitzgerald (b 1918), Nat King Cole (b 1919), Mel Torme (b 1925) and Ray Charles (b 1930).

Chuck Berry

Henry Mancini

...helped create the new sound.

Many of the original rock 'n' roll bands of the 1960s were inspired by the postwar rhythm and blues performers including Muddy Waters (b 1915), B.B. King (b 1925), Bo Diddley (b 1928), Chuck Berry (b 1926), and Fats Domino (b 1928). Considered equally important to the development of rock 'n' roll is guitar-maker Leo Fender (b 1908), whose patented guitars helped create the new sound.

There were also exceptional songwriters, composers, and conductors from the WWII generation whose works will remain revered. These include Stephen Sondheim (b 1930), the author of popular musical plays, conductor Leonard Bernstein (b 1918), Sammy Cahn (b 1913), who wrote numerous memorable songs, and composer and conductor Henry Mancini (b 1924).

Ray Charles

…future generations will be paying their own tribute…

The very popular country music genre also has deep roots in the American WWII generation. Roy Acuff (b 1903) was the Grand Ol' Opry's first singing star and is known by many as the "King of Country Music." Another pioneer was Eddy Arnold (b 1918), who made so many radio appearances in the 1940s that many urban dwellers became country music fans. Guitarist Chet Atkins (b 1907, Tex Ritter (b 1907), Ernest Tubb (b 1914), who is credited with developing the honky-tonk style so prevelent today, and hard-living Hank Williams (b 1923) are also immortals of country music. An innovative new style of country music was started by the "Father of Bluegrass," Bill Monroe (b 1911).

The continued enjoyment of the WWII generation music by successive generations, including today's generation X, shows what truly great music it is. This music will never fade, and that is good news because future generations will be paying their own tribute to the WWII generation every time they play one of the unforgettable songs from these unforgettable song writers and singers.

$\mathcal{M}$otion pictures

Of all the members of the American WWII generation, probably none will be remembered as well as the film stars whose films remain very popular around the world today. Just a few of these immortals include Charlton Heston (b 1924), Orson Wells (b 1915), Henry Fonda (b 1905), Jerry Lewis (b 1926), Gene Kelley (b 1912), Clark Gable (b 1901), Fred Astaire (b 1899), Ginger Rogers (b 1911), Gene Autry (b 1907), Cary Grant (b 1906), Katharine Hepburn (b 1907), Kirk Douglas (b 1916), Paul Newman (b 1925), Marilyn Monroe (b 1926), Marlon Brando (b 1924), and Jack Lemmon (b 1925).

Some other film immortals made military films for the war effort long before they became famous. These included director John Houston (b 1906) who was a major, executive Darryl F. Zanuck (b 1902), a lieutenant, and Jimmy Stewart (b 1908), who flew many missions over Germany as a fighter pilot. The father of film animation, Walt Disney (b 1901), made many morale-boosting

Walt Disney

films, and his company volunteered to design many insignias for the armed services. Perhaps the most popular Hollywood person of all time was John Wayne (b 1907), who was renowned for his patriotism both on and off the big screen.

The movies made with these and many other stars, too numerous too list, did more for creating an impression and understanding of American culture for the rest of the world than any other means. Today, American film-making remains the dominant force in the distribution of films around the world, and much of this is due to the popularity of the WWII legends. A lot of credit must also be given to those nameless WWII generation creative and technical people behind the camera who kept America at the top of the profession by rapidly advancing the art and science of film-making.

American Academy Award Winners from the WWII generation:

1931 Helen Hayes (b 1900) Best Actress: *The Sin of Madelon Claudet*

1932 Katharine Hepburn (b 1907) Best Actress: *Morning Glory*

1934 Clark Gable (b 1901) Best Actor: *It Happened One Night*

1935 Bette Davis (b 1908) Best Actress: *Dangerous*

1938 Bette Davis (b 1908) Best Actress: *Jezebel*

1940 Jimmy Stewart (b 1908) Best Actor: *The Philadelphia Story*

1941 Gary Cooper (b 1901) Best Actor: *Sergeant York*

1943 Jennifer Jones (b 1919) Best Actress: *The Song of Bernadette*

1944 Bing Crosby (b 1904) Best Actor: *Going My Way*

1945 Joan Crawford (b 1904) Best Actress: *Mildred Pierce*

1946 William Wyler (b 1902) Best Director: *The Best Years of Our Lives*

1947 Elia Kazen (b 1909) Best Director: *Gentlemen's Agreement*

1947 Loretta Young (b 1913) Best Actress: *The Farmer's Daughter*

American Academy Award Winners from the WWII generation: *(cont.)*

Best Director & Best Actor or Actress:

1948   John Houston (b 1906) Best Director: *The Treasure of Sierra Madre*

1948   Jane Wyman (b 1914) Best Actress: *Johnny Belinda*

1949   Joseph L. Mankiewicz (b 1909) Best Director: *A Letter to Three Wives*

1950   Jose Ferrer (b 1909) Best Actor: *Cyrano de Bergerac*

1950   Judy Holliday (b 1922) Best Actress: *Born Yesterday*

1951   George Stevens (b 1904) Best Director: *A Place in the Sun*

1952   Gary Cooper (b 1901) Best Actor: *High Noon*

1952   Shirley Booth (b 1907) Best Actress: *Come Back Little Sheba*

1953   William Holden (b 1918) Best Actor: *Stalig 17*

1954   Elia Kazen (b 1909) Best Director: *On The Waterfront*

1954   Marlon Brando (b 1924) Best Actor: *On The Waterfront*

1954   Grace Kelly (b 1928) Best Actress: *The Country Girl*

1955   Delbert Mann (b 1920) Best Director: *Marty*

1955   Ernest Borgnine (b 1917) Best Actor: *Marty*

American Academy Award Winners from the WWII generation: *(cont.)*

Best Director & Best Actor or Actress:

1956 George Stevens (b 1904) Best Director: *Giant*

1957 Joanne Woodward (b 1930) Best Actress: *The Three Faces of Eve*

1958 Vincette Minelli (b 1910) Best Director: *Gigi*

1958 Susan Hayward (b 1918) Best Actress: *I Want to Live*

1959 Charlton Heston (b 1923) Best Actor: *Ben Hur*

1960 Burt Lancaster (b 1913) Best Actor: *Elmer Gantry*

Charlton Heston

Sidney Poitier

American Academy Award Winners from the WWII generation: *(cont.)*

Best Director & Best Actor or Actress:

1961   Jeane Robbins (b 1918) Best Director: *West Side Story*

1961   Robert Wise (b 1914) Best Director: *West Side Story*

1962   Gregory Peck (b 1916) Best Actor: *To Kill A Mockingbird*

1963   Sydney Poitier (b 1924) Best Actor: *Lilies of the Field*

1963   Patricia Neal (b 1926) Best Actress: *Hud*

1965   Robert Wise (b 1914) Best Director: *The Sound Of Music*

John Wayne

Best Director & Best Actor or Actress:

1965 Lee Marvin (b 1924) Best Actor: *Cat Ballou*

1967 Rod Steiger (b 1925) Best Actor: *In The Heat Of The Night*

1967 Katharine Hepburn (b 1907) Best Actress: *Guess Who's Coming To Dinner?*

1968 Cliff Robertson (b 1925) Best Actor: *Charly*

1968 Katharine Hepburn (b 1907) Best Actress: *The Lion in Winter*

1969 John Wayne (b 1907) Best Actor: *True Grit*

1970 George C. Scott (b 1927) Best Actor: *Patton*

1972 Bob Fosse (b 1927) Best Director: *Cabaret*

1972 Marlon Brando (b 1924) Best Actor: *The Godfather*

1973 George Redhill (b 1922) Best Director: *The Sting*

1973 Jack Lemmon (b 1925) Best Actor: *Save the Tiger*

1974 Art Carney (b 1918) Best Actor: *Harry and Tonto*

1981 Henry Fonda (b 1905) Best Actor: *On Golden Pond*

1981 Katharine Hepburn (b 1907) Best Actress: *On Golden Pond*

1985 Geraldine Page (b 1924) Best Actress: *The Trip To Bountiful*

1986 Paul Newman (b 1925) Best Actor: *The Color Of Money*

Jack Lemmon

American Academy Award Winners: Best Supporting Actress or Actor

1941   Mary Astor (b 1906) *The Great Lie*

1942   Van Heflin (b 1910) *Johnny Eager*

1942   Theresa Wright (b 1918) *Mrs. Miniver*

1945   James Dunn (b 1905) *A Tree Grows In Brooklyn*

1945   Anne Revere (b 1903) *National Velvet*

1946   Harold Russell (b 1914) *The Best Years Of Our Lives*

1946   Anne Baxter (b 1923) *The Razor's Edge*

1947   Celest Holm (b 1919) *Gentelman's Agreement*

1948   Claire Trevor (b 1909) *Key Largo*

1949   Dean Jagger (b 1903) *Twelve O'clock High*

1949   Mercedes McCaimbridge (b 1918) *All The Kings Men*

1951   Karl Malden (b 1914) *A Streetcar Named Desire*

1951   Kim Hunter (b 1922) *A Streetcar Named Desire*

1952   Gloria Graham (b 1925) *The Bad And The Beautiful*

1953   Frank Sinatra (b 1915) *From Here To Eternity*

1953   Donna Reed (b 1921) *From Here To Eternity*

1954   Edmond O'Brien (b 1915) *The Barefoot Contessa*

1954   Eva Marie Saint (b 1924) *On The Waterfront*

1955   Jack Lemmon (b 1925) *Mister Roberts*

1955   Jo Van Fleet (b 1919) *East Of Eden*

1956   Dorothy Malone (b 1925) *Written On The Wind*

1957   Red Buttons (b 1919) *Sayanora*

1958   Burl Ives (b 1909) *The Big Country*

1959   Shelly Winters (b 1922) *The Diary Of Anne Frank*

1962   Ed Begley (b 1901) *Sweet Bird of Youth*

1963   Melvyn Douglas (b 1901) *Hud*

1966   Walter Matthau (b 1920) *The Fortune Cookie*

1967   George Kennedy (b 1925) *Cool Hand Luke*

1967   Estelle Parsons (b 1927) *Bonnie and Clyde*

1968   Jack Albertson (b 1910) *The Subject Was Roses*

1969   Gig Young (b 1913) *They Shoot Horses Don't They?*

1970   Helen Hughes (b 1900) *Airport*

1971   Ben Johnson (b 1920) *The Big Picture Show*

1971   Cloris Leachman (b 1926) *The Big Picture Show*

1972   Eileen Heckart (b 1919) *Butterflies Are Free*

1976   Jason Robards (b 1922) *Julia*

1979   Melvyn Douglas (b 1901) *Being There*

1981   Maureen Stapelton (b 1925) *Reds*

1985   Don Ameche (b 1908) *Cocoon*

1991   Jack Palance (b 1919) *City Slickers*

*T*elevision

In 1927 Utah engineer Philo Taylor Farnsworth (b 1906) invented something that would forever change America and the world. It was called the electric television. In 1945 only about 5000 American homes had television and there wasn't much programming available.

American families would gather together to watch television's original programming, including Arthur Godfrey (b 1903), "Mr. Television," Milton Berle (b 1908), Ted Mack (b 1904) and his *Original Amateur Hour,* Art Linkletter (b 1912), comedian Red Skelton (b 1913), and Ed Sullivan (b 1901). By 1950 approximately five million homes had television. By this time, there was also much more programming available, as over one hundred television stations were in operation.

Among this new programming were the shows that most baby boomers shall never forget, including *Howdy Doody,* created by Buffalo Bob Smith (b 1917), who also created characters such as Fluba Dub, Dolly Dolly, Princess Summerfall-Winterspring, and others. The other most popular children's show of this era was the *Kukla, Fran, and Ollie Show*, with puppeteers Fran Allison (b 1908) and Burr Tillstrom (b 1917). Disney's weekly show started in 1954, and 1955 brought us the *Captain Kangaroo Show* starring host Robert Keeshan (b 1927).

Other WWII generation legends that baby boomers will remember are Lucille Ball (b 1912) and her husband Desi Arnez (b 1917) in *I Love Lucy*, Sid Caesar (b 1922), Imogene Coca (b 1908) Andy Griffith (b 1926), Dick Van Dyke (b 1925), Jackie Gleason (b 1916), and Jack Webb (b 1920), whose television show *Dragnet* was the prototype for all police shows.

Lucille Ball

Shows about American families were quite popular. The most popular was *Leave It To Beaver* which premiered in 1957 and lasted until 1963. This show featured Hugh Beaumont (b 1909) and Barbara Billingsley (b 1922). Other popular family shows were *The Donna Reed Show,* staring Donna Reed (b 1921), *My Three Sons*, starring Fred McMurray (b 1908), which ran from 1960 until 1972, and *The Andy Griffith Show* with Andy Griffith (b 1926).

Some of the most popular television actors, enjoyed by young and old alike, were those who played in dramas of the American West. The first was the singing cowboy, Gene Autry (b1907). Later, there was Clayton Moore (b 1908), who starred in *The Lone Ranger*, and the team of Roy Rogers (b 1911) and Dale Evans (b 1912). *Bonanza*, starring Lorne Green (b 1915), lasted from 1959 to 1973, and James Arness (b 1928) starred in *Gunsmoke,* which ran for an amazing twenty years after it premiered in 1955.

As the baby boomers matured, television started to change also. In 1967 one of America's first non-traditional programs, *Rowan and Martin's Laugh In,* premiered. This show featured hosts Dan Rowan (b 1922) and Dick Martin (b 1923) with a cast of zany comedic characters. It lasted until 1973. In 1971 Producer Norman Lear (b 1922) introduced *All in the Family,* which was considered quite controversial because it dealt with sensitive, mature situations in humorous ways. After a very slow start, this show, starring Carol O'Connor (b 1924) as Archie Bunker, became an American favorite for many years.

Other WWII generation television legends that will be remembered for their professionalism are newsmen Walter Cronkite (b 1917), Chet Huntley (b 1911), and David Brinkley (b 1920). Whether it was the tragic news of assassinations, when they kept their composure for the good of the nation, or during the wonder of the landing on the moon, they led the rest of us in the best way possible.

Perhaps the two most popular television personalities from the WWII generation were Johnny Carson (b 1925) known as the "King of Late Night," and USO performer Bob Hope (b 1903), who provided countless good memories with his specials.

All of these television entertainers and many others were a big part of the baby boomer's growing up, as television became a large factor in American culture. Not only were the entertainers talented, but the programming was considered a very positive influence on the youth of America. This is why most baby boomers recall nothing but good childhood memories from television while growing up. The good intentions of the WWII generation talent and programmers will always be appreciated by the baby boomers.

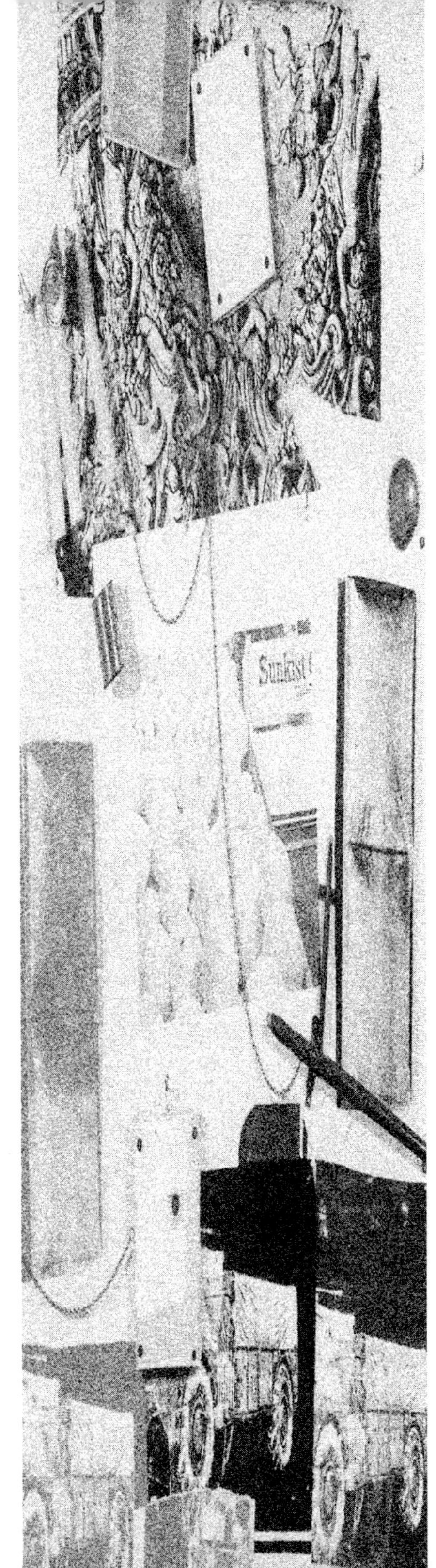

Art

In the late 1930s, the art center of the world was changing from Paris to New York City. For the first time, a genuine art movement was originating in the United States. It was called Abstract Expressionism or "action painting." Its recognition by the art world was slow to develop as most museums were still showcasing "realistic" art. In 1940 some of the abstract artists even picketed the museum of modern art demanding the museum display American art. Only after a few museums, including the Museum of Living Art, the Dudensing Gallery, and the Solomon R. Guggenheim Museum of Non-objective Art, agreed to display the new form did it catch on. Many experts agreed that abstract art was the best way for artists to express the new technological age that was starting in the post-World War II ear. Among those American artists who deserve credit for the modern art movement are Franz Kline (b 1910), Robert Motherwell (b 1915), Jack Tworkov (b 1900), Kenneth Nolan (b 1924), and John Chamberlin (b 1927).

Also given credit for America's new-found respect in world art was Wyoming born, Jackson Pollock (b 1912). Pollock combined both the abstract and expressionism to create some critically acclaimed "drip" paintings that are considered quite historic today.

By the 1960s, two new identifiable styles had been created. These were called "new abstraction" and "pop art." Pop art was a very unique American style that expressed American culture. The most famous American artist known for this style is Andy Warhol (b 1928), who became an international celebrity. Some of his most famous paintings portrayed Campbell's soup cans and bottles of Coca-Cola. Other well known pop artists include Roy Lichtenstein (b 1923) and Robert Rauschenberg (b 1925), the latter did a number of paintings of the presidents of the 1960s.

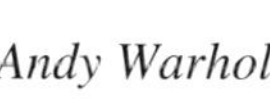

Andy Warhol

Charles Schultz

Another form of art was newspaper comic strips. Most baby boomers can remember picking up the paper to see such strips as *L'il Abner* by Al Cap (b 1909), *Dennis the Menace* by Hank Ketchum (b 1920), and *Superman,* created by Joe Shuster (b 1914) and Jerome Siegel (b 1914). Perhaps the most popular of the comics was *Peanuts,* done by the legendary Charles Shultz (b 1922).

No matter what direction the art of the WWII generation took, it will not be forgotten: History shows that the world cherished it, no matter how complex or simple it might have been.

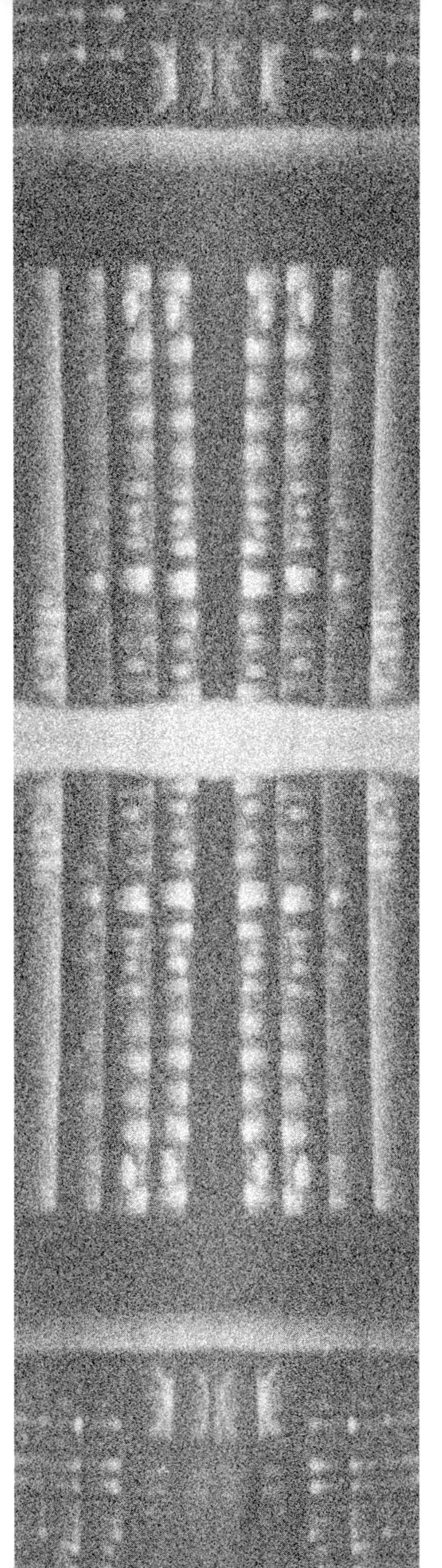

Literature

Much of the great literature written by WWII generation writers was about American life as it evolved right in front of the writer's eyes. Many great writers from this generation were veterans of WWII and Korea, and this inspired their stories. An example of this was Norman Mailer (b 1923), who joined the US Army in 1944 and wrote many stories related to the military. James Michener (b 1907) served in the navy during WWII where he wrote his famous *Tales of the South Pacific.* He went on to write numerous best sellers set in locations all over the world.

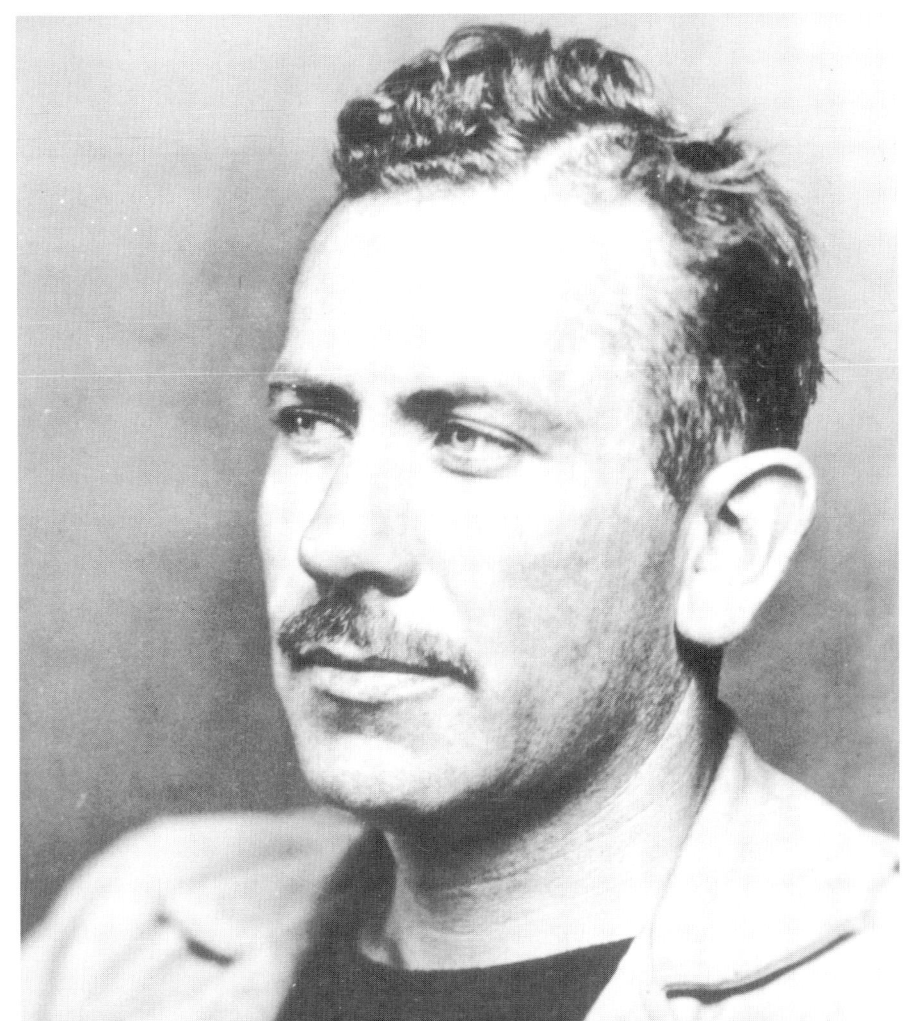

Literary giant John Steinbeck (b 1902) wrote a famous story about the despair of the 1930s that became a movie classic, *The Grapes of Wrath*. Steinbeck is also known for other writings of realism and romanticism. He was the seventh American-born author to win a Nobel Prize. Other notable fiction writers from the WWII generation were James Jones (b 1921), Gore Vidal (b 1925), Kurt Vonnegut (b 1922), Truman Capote (b 1924), and science fiction pioneer Ray Bradbury (b 1920).

Tennessee Williams

Norman Mailer

The two most respected playwrights from the WWII generation were Tennessee Williams (b 1911) and Arthur Miller (b 1915). William's dramas *The Glass Menagerie* and *A Streetcar Named Desire* are American Classics, as is Miller's *Death of a Salesman*.

American poetry, like the other forms of art after World War II, was affected by a modern movement in verse and style. Memorable poems came from Theodore Roethke (b 1908), Elizabeth Bishop (b 1911), and Richard Wilbur (b 1921). Considered to be the most heartbreaking poet of the whole generation was Randell Jarrell (b 1914). Much of his poetry was about the tribulations of the war. His poem called "The Death of the Ball Turret Gunner" is an exceptional example of his work.

Sports

There hasn't been a more significant moment in athletic history than on baseball's opening day in 1947 when Jackie Roosevelt Robinson (b 1919) became the first black player to compete in the major leagues. After enduring much hardship in his first year, he was nonetheless voted the National League Rookie of the Year. This paved the way for many other black players, not only in baseball, but in all of the professional sports. Many felt this was a giant step towards the legislation for equality that was passed in later years.

Jackie Robinson

Naturally, during WWII most of the national concern was on winning the war. During this period most of the national heroes were military or government figures. But soon after the war ended America experienced a wave of sports enthusiasm. There were many great athletic feats accomplished by members of the WWII generation in all sports including Olympic competition. It would be very difficult to name them all, but in chronological order the major ones are listed in the following pages.

1936 Jesse Owens (b 1913) wins four gold medals at the Berlin Olympics in defiance of Adolph Hitler, the German host who believed in white supremacy. Hitler left the stadium after each of Owens' victories so he didn't have to present medals to Owens.

1937 Joe Louis (b 1914) gains the world heavyweight championship; he kept it for a record twelve years.

1938 Don Budge (b 1915) is the first to win the first Grand Slam in tennis, which wouldn't be repeated by anyone for twenty-four years.

1941 Joe Dimaggio (b 1914) has a record 56-game hitting streak, a record that has never been broken. He led the Yankees to ten World Series titles as a centerfielder.

Ted Williams

1941 Ted Williams (b 1918) had a .406 batting average and is still the last man to hit over .400. He won the Most Valualbe Player Award twice and missed all or part of five seasons due to military service as a Marine combat pilot in WWII and Korea.

1941–1945 Most American athletes, including top professionals, joined the Armed Forces in an effort to win World War II. Most sporting events were suspended.

1945 George Mikan (b 1924) from DePaul University scores 120 points in three games to be named the NIT's most valuable player. He later went on to lead the Minneapolis Lakers to four NBA championships and in 1997 was named one of the NBA's top fifty players of all time.

1946 Sam Snead (b 1912) wins the first British Open played since 1939, when the war had interrupted play. In his career, he won an all-time record 81 PGA tour victories including three Masters and three PGA championships.

Stan Musial

1947 Jack Kramer (b 1921) wins the Wimbledon singles tennis championship.

1948 Stan Musial (b 1920) is named baseball's Most Valuable Player for the third time.

1951 Bobby Thompson (b 1924) hits a 3-run home run in the bottom of the ninth inning of a baseball playoff game to win the pennant for the New York Giants over the Brooklyn Dodgers.

1952 Sammy Baugh (b 1914) retires after fifteen years as quarterback with the Washington Redskins. He led the NFL in passing six times and in punting four times.

1952 Bob Mathias (b 1930) is the first person to repeat as Olympic decathlon champion.

1953 Bobby Layne (b 1927) quarterbacks the Detroit Lions to a repeat NFL championship.

1953 Ben Hogan (b 1912) wins the US Open and the British Open, and then the Masters by five strokes, a record. Today, he remains the only person to have won three of the four Grand Slam golf events in one year.

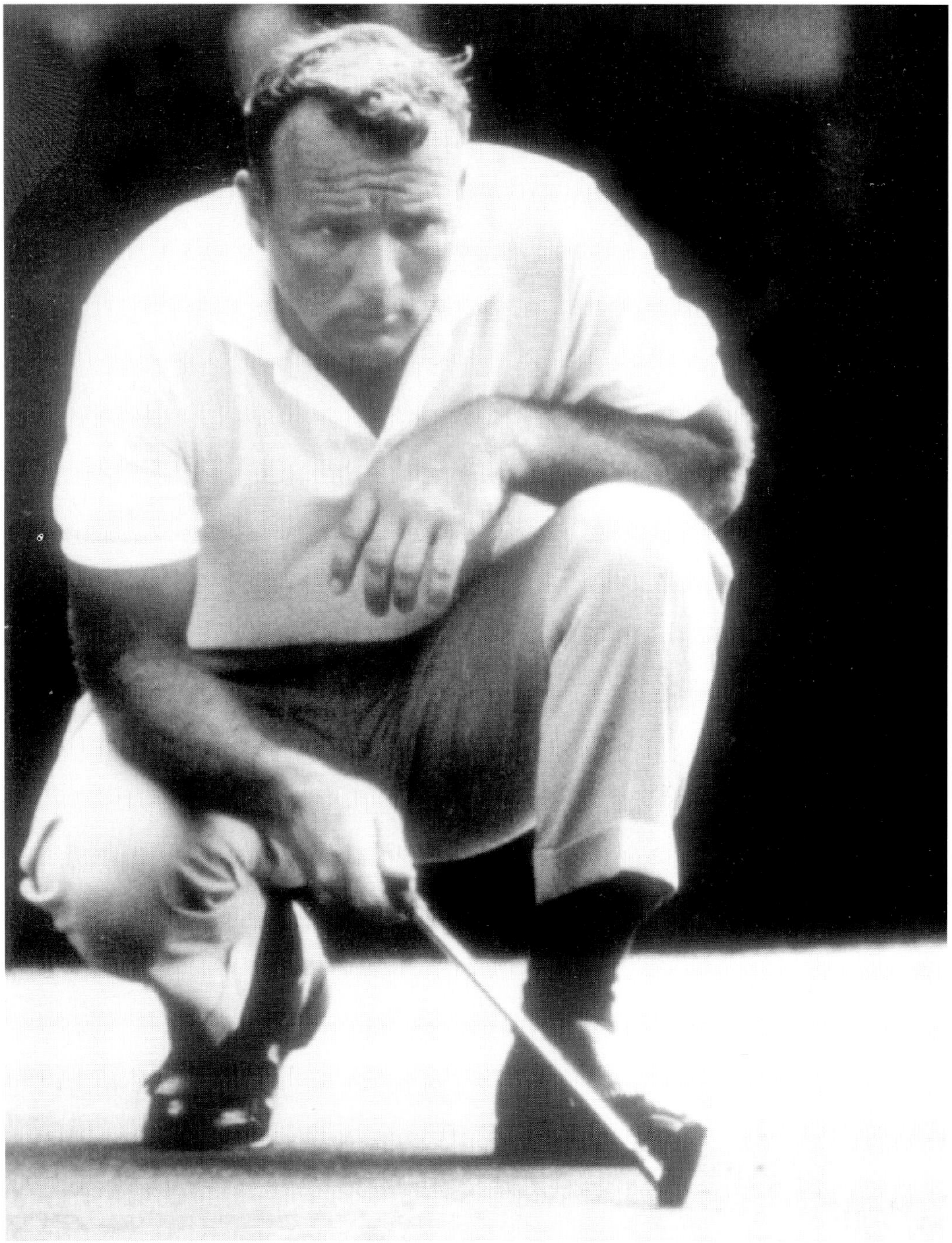

Arnold Palmer

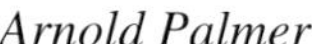

1954 Bill Vukovich (b 1927) becomes only the third person to win back to back Indianapolis 500 car races. He died in the 1955 race trying to win a never-been-done third straight.

1956 Don Larson (b 1929) pitches the first and only perfect game in World Series baseball history.

1956 Archie Moore (b 1914), at the age of forty-two, loses his heavyweight boxing title to Floyd Patterson.

Sugar Ray Robinson

1957 Middleweight boxing champion Sugar Ray Robinson (b 1921) loses the title in January, reclaims it in May, and loses it again in September, all at the age of thirty-six.

1958 Arnold Palmer (b 1930) wins his first Masters golf tournament. He would go on to win two more Masters, three US Opens, and two British Opens, and would become one of the most popular golfers of all time.

1958 Adolph Rupp (b 1917) coaches the University of Kentucky basketball team to a fourth and final NCAA championship during his tenure as coach from 1931 to 1972.

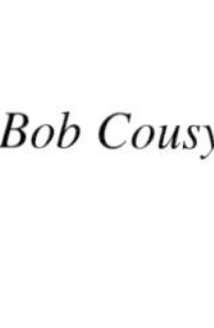

Bob Cousy

1959 Four-time all-pro footballer Ollie Matson (b 1930) is traded by the Chicago Cardinals to the L.A. Rams for eight players.

1960 Pete Rozelle (b 1926) becomes the commissioner of the National Football League, where he served until 1989.

1961 New York Yankee pitcher Whitey Ford (b 1928) wins the World Series and the Cy Young Award.

1961 Bob Cousy (b 1928) was named to the National Basketball Association's First Team for the tenth straight year.

1962 Y.A. Tittle (b 1926) of the New York football Giants is named the Most Valuable Player for the second time.

1962 Yogi Berra (b 1925) wins his tenth and final World Series as a New York Yankee.

1964 Paul Bear Bryant (b 1913) leads his University of Alabama football team to the second of five national championships during his tenure as coach from 1958 to 1982.

1965 Bowler Dick Weber (b 1929) wins his third and final PBA Bowler of the Year award.

1965 Satchel Paige (b 1906), at age fifty-nine, pitches a baseball game in the major leagues, giving up only one hit in three innings.

Vince Lombardi

Red Auerbach

1966   Red Auerbach (b 1917) coaches the Boston Celtics to their eighth title in a row and retires. He won a record total of nine championships in twenty seasons as coach.

1967   Coach Vince Lombardi (b 1913) and his Green Bay Packers win the first Super Bowl ever played and would go on to win the following year as well.

1968   Woody Hayes (b 1913) leads the Ohio State Buckeyes to their third and final national championship in college football. He coached Ohio State from 1951 to 1978.

Johnny Wooden

1970 Bob Devaney (b 1915) coaches the Nebraska Cornhuskers to their first national championship and repeats the feat the following year. He coached Nebraska from 1962 to 1972.

1972 George Blanda (b 1927) ends his illustrious NFL career where he played a record twenty-six years.

1973 Bobby Riggs (b 1918) loses in three straight sets to Billie Jean King in the Battle of the Sexes tennis match.

1975 Johnny Wooden (b 1910) coach of the UCLA basketball Bruins wins his tenth and final NCAA championship. He had won nine championships the previous eleven years. He coached UCLA from 1949 to 1975. He is the only person elected to the college basketball Hall of Fame as both a player and a coach.

1976 Manager Walter Alston retires (b 1911) after managing the Brooklyn–L.A. Dodgers for twenty-three years, winning seven pennants and four World Series.

1978 Coach Tom Landry (b 1924) wins his second and final Super Bowl. He went on to coach another ten years.

James Counsilman

1979 James "Doc" Counsilman (b 1920) became the oldest person to successfully swim the English Channel.

1981 Manager Tommy Lasorda (b 1927) of the Los Angeles Dodgers leads his team to their first World Series championship with him at the helm. He would win one more in 1988, and would retire in 1996 after twenty-one years as manager.

1986 Coach Joe Paterno (b 1926) and his Penn State college football team wins the national champion-ship. He also had three unbeaten teams that didn't finish number one along with his other championship in 1982. The 1997 campaign was his thirty-first season.

...the
voices of
baseball
from the
1950's
to the
1990's.

1991 Walter Red Barber (b 1908) wins the Peabody Award for radio commentary. He, along with Mel Allen (b 1913), Harry Caray (b 1914), Vin Scully (b 1927), and Jack Buck (b 1925) will be remembered as the voices of baseball from the 1950s to the 1990s.

Walter
"Red"
Barber

Mel Allen

Vin Scully

Harry Caray

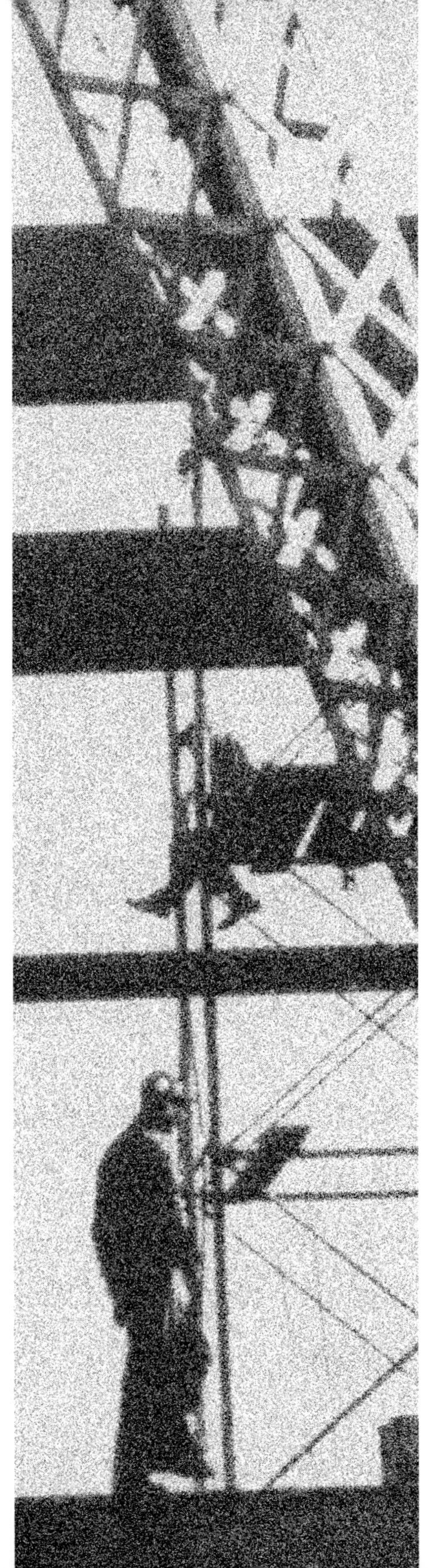

Work ethic
building modern America

After WWII, many experts expected the American economy to fall rapidly into a deep recession like most of Europe did. Not only did the US economy avoid this—but it produced as much as it did in the previous 350 years!

Miners in a coal mine.

The postwar period saw the United States become the most affluent country in the world, and it happened rather quickly. Between 1945 and 1961, the gross national product was up 60 percent and the distribution of wealth was improving. Some of the major unions, including auto and steel, were successful in obtaining higher wages. The huge demand of goods and services from the young families of those who fought in WWII grew and grew. In 1955 US automobile plants were manufacturing almost eight million cars a year, and approximately 1.3 million trucks and buses. Another major part of the growth was the new interstate highway system. Construction started in 1956 and it had a tremendous impact on the social lives of Americans—how they chose where to work, live, shop, and vacation.

The factor that most influenced America's growth during this period was the "hard-work ethic." Unlike the many technological careers of today, most of the work building postwar America was manufacturing—houses, automobiles, steel, bridges, skyscrapers, new roads, and so on—which required difficult, dangerous, hands-on work.

Throughout America's history, previous generations also worked extremely hard, but it would be difficult to imagine a harder-working generation than the one that literally built modern America with their own hands. The blue-collar worker is *the* single most important figure from this generation, more important than any famous individual from big business, politics, or sports. America would not have become the country it did without their contribution. *A Tribute to Our Parents* is especially dedicated to these people who never requested or received the credit they deserved.

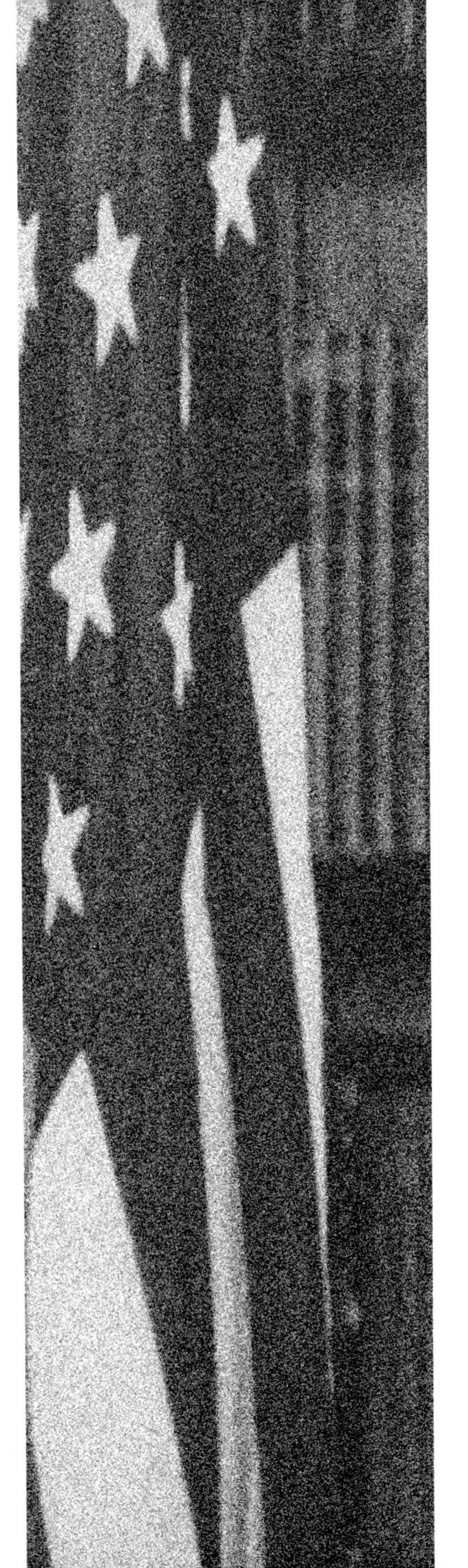

*L*eaders

United States Presidents

John F. Kennedy (b 1917)

After the 1960 election, he proclaimed in his inaugural address "to friend and foe alike, that the torch has been passed to a new generation of Americans born in this century," seeming at that moment to officially become the first WWII generation president. For his service as a PT boat commander in the United States Navy from 1941 to 1945, he was awarded a Purple Heart and the Navy and Marine Corps medals. He was a US congressman from 1947 to 1953, and a US senator from 1958 to 1960. He was the youngest man ever elected president. Among his most noted accomplishments were leading the space race to the moon, helping advance civil rights, and during one of the most tense times in world history, resolving the Cuban missile crisis.

Lyndon B Johnson (b 1908)

He served as a US congressman from 1937 to 1949 with a temporary leave to serve in the US Navy in 1941 and 1942. Elected a US senator from 1949 to 1961, he was majority leader from 1955 until he became vice president in January 1961 and ran the Presidential Committee of Equal Employment. In 1963 he took over as president after the Kennedy assassination and in 1964 was elected president himself. He was most known for his Civil Rights Bill of 1964 and for his social welfare programs. Among these were the Social Security Amendment of 1965, which created Medicare and Medicaid.

Richard M. Nixon (b 1913)

He was in the US Navy from 1942 to 1946 and became a lieutenant commander. He served as a US congressman from 1947 to 1951 and was elected a US senator in 1951. He then became the vice president from 1953 to 1961. After his 1968 presidential election victory, he distinguished himself as the man who opened up US–China foreign relations during a trip in 1972. Later that year he established "détente," as the first President to visit the Soviet Union since 1945. He was also known as the "Father of Title IX," a crucial law to improve opportunities for women collegiate athletes, and he had many concerns for the environment. Also, President Nixon was a big supporter of the space shuttle program, and he signed a bill for construction of the Alaskan pipeline to help reduce America's dependence on foreign oil.

Gerald Ford (b 1913)

President Ford was in the US Navy from 1941 to 1945. He was a US congressman from 1948 to 1972, and he served as the House minority leader from 1965 to 1972. In 1972 he became vice president after the previous vice president resigned. He became president in 1974 after the resignation of Richard Nixon and is best known as the "healer" of the country after the Watergate scandal. After serving successfully in the US House for many years, he was known as a man of exceptional integrity. He signed a campaign reform bill in 1974 that was the first of its kind and insisted on reform of the US intelligence agencies (CIA, FBI) because of alleged abuses on American citizens. He also made some significant strides in "detente" with the Soviet Union.

Jimmy Carter (b 1924)

President Carter attended the US Naval Academy from 1943 to 1946 and served in the Navy until 1953. He became a Georgia state senator in 1963 and served until 1966. He lost the race for governor in 1966, but won in 1970. He became president in 1976. He is best known as the key negotiator in the Camp David Agreement between Israel and Egypt in 1978, and he was also a strong advocate for civil rights. Since leaving office after his re-election loss in 1980, he has continued to be very active in world affairs as an American diplomat and has supported many causes for the poor of America. He is regarded as a highly moral man whose integrity is impeccable.

Ronald Reagan (b 1911)

A member of the Army Reserve during WWII, he was not allowed in combat because of poor eyesight. He made training films for the Screen Actors Guild during 1947 to 1952 and 1959 to 1960. As a leading man in television and film, he became a well-recognized figure and decided to become more involved in politics. He was elected governor of California in 1966 and became known as a "tax cutter" and a conservative, after previously being considered a liberal. After losing the Republican presidential nominations in 1968 and in 1976, his unmatched determination finally paid off when he won the 1980 presidential election. His plans to reduce government and taxes worked well—the recession ended, inflation was reduced significantly, and a record number of new jobs were created. His strong

pro-military and anti-Communist opinions and his ability to negotiate a 1987 Nuclear Disarmament Treaty with the Soviet Union were also popular. Many people give him major credit for the collapse of Communism in the 1980s. Not only was he the oldest president ever elected, but was also the most popular since WWII.

George Bush (b 1924)

He enlisted in the US Naval Reserve in 1943 and became the Navy's youngest pilot. He was awarded the Distinguished Flying Cross for being shot down by the Japanese and rescued by a submarine shortly before being captured. After returning home, he went to Texas where he became quite successful in the oil business. He became a US congressman in 1967 and lost a Senate bid in 1970. He became a US ambassador to the United Nations in 1971, the chief liaison to China in 1974, and CIA director in 1976. He became Reagan's vice president in 1980. After being a very loyal vice president, he won his own presidential bid in 1988. He was most noted for his foreign policy expertise. This included his skillful leadership of the US-led coalition in Desert Storm (1991) and his handling of the end of the Cold War and the collapse of the Soviet Union. He was the last president of the WWII generation. When he lost the election to Bill Clinton in 1990, the torch passed to another generation, just as it had in 1960.

Other leaders

From the
WWII Generation

Robert Dole
(b 1923)

Dole was a war hero who almost died of the injuries he received during the invasion of northern Italy in WWII. He became a US congressman from Kansas in 1961, and served until 1969 when he became a US senator. He served as Senate majority leader in 1981 until 1987 and again in 1994 when Republicans regained control of the Senate. For many years, his leadership in Congress was instrumental in passing much major legislation. He resigned in 1996 when he ran for president. When Senator Dole lost the presidential election, it meant a likely end to the WWII generation presidents and the closing of a chapter of American history.

Betty Friedan
(b 1921)

Ms. Friedan was a psychologist who concluded that women were unfulfilled by their place in American society. She wrote *The Feminine Mystique* to convey her strong feelings, and she was one of the founders of the National Organization Of Women, where she served as president from its inception in 1966 until 1970.

Billy Graham
(b 1918)

He began his evangelistic campaigns in 1946, and they still continue today. He was a good friend to many US presidents and has inspired millions of people over the years. He is one of the most popular Americans from the WWII generation.

Kathleen Graham
(b 1917)

After her husband's death in 1963, she ran the Washington Post Company, which included the newspaper, major magazines, and some television stations. She was one of the most powerful women in the country from the middle 1960s until her resignation as chairman of the board in 1991. Her biography, "Personal History," won a Pulitzer Prize in 1998.

Bob Hope
(b 1903)

He started his career as a vaudevillian and went on to stage, movie, and television where he became an American institution. He was best known as the man who went to the front lines to entertain the troops from WWII to Desert Storm. Many polls have shown him as the WWII generation's most popular individual.

 **Hubert H. Humphrey
(b 1911)**

A US Senate leader from 1948 until his death in 1978, except during 1964 to 1968 when he was vice president, he was known as a liberal man with progressive ideas and a friend of the Civil Rights movement. He was always known as an honorable man. Many don't realize that he and Richard Nixon, to whom he lost the 1968 Presidential election, had a very close friendship for many years before and after that contest. He played a major role in much of the legislation passed from 1950 to the 1970s.

Martin Luther King (b 1929)

A son and grandson of Baptist Ministers in Atlanta, Georgia, King formed the Southern Christian Leadership Conference, a leading organization in the civil rights movement of the 1950s and 1960s. He led the nonviolent protests prevalent during those years and was awarded the Nobel Peace Prize in 1964. He was assassinated in 1968, but his ideology has been carried on by his followers. King's "I have a dream…" speech in Washington, D.C., in 1963 will remain one of the most notorious speeches in American history.

Henry Kissinger (b 1923)

He was one of the most respected and efficient statesman in American history. He was born in Germany and served in the American army during WWII. The Nobel Peace Prize was awarded to him in 1973 for his role in ending the Vietnam War. He also served as President Ford's secretary of state and has remained a willing outside consultant on many foreign policy issues since leaving the government in 1976.

Thurgood Marshall
(b 1908)

He was the victorious leading attorney in the famous Brown vs. the Board of Education of Topeka case in 1954. Nominated in 1961for the U.S. Court of Appeals, and subsequently as Solicitor General in 1965, Marshall was the first black person to become a United States Supreme Court judge. He was a very active leading jurist during one of the most activist times of the Court, from the late 1960s until his retirement in 1991.

Sandra Day O'Conner
(b 1930)

She graduated from Stanford Law School from in 1952, then moved to Germany during her husband's service in the Army. She moved to Arizona in 1957 to practice law, and by the 1960s, she had become a state assistant attorney general, and then the Arizona Senate majority leader in 1973. Shortly afterwards, she took a position as an Arizona Supreme Court judge and in 1981 was nominated by President Ronald Reagan as the first female US Supreme Court justice.

J. Robert Oppenheimer
(b 1904)

He was the director of the Los Alamos Science Laboratory in 1942 and chairman of the advisory committee of the Atomic Energy Commission. He is known as the "Father of the Atomic Bomb." His plan for international control of atomic energy was widely known. In 1963 he won a Fermi Prize for his contributions to physics.

Jackie Robinson
(b 1919)

A grandson of a slave, he was the first black man to play baseball in the major leagues. As difficult as it was, he somehow refused to let frequent harassment destroy him and what he represented. He prevailed, not only helping other players of color, but also greatly helping the Civil Rights movement that followed.

Dr. Jonas Salk
(b 1914)

He received his medical degree from NYU in 1939. Following his graduation he worked for the Army on a vaccine to combat influenza, which eventually proved successful. During the 1940s he headed a research team to find a cure for the horrendous polio disease. By 1953 he had found a vaccine, and by 1955 millions of people were saved. Up until his death in 1996, he was still working feverishly to find an AIDS cure. He refused to take any personal profit for his work.

Baby boomers

It would be quite foolish and complex to try to rate the major accomplishments of the WWII generation, but one thing that is for sure is that the baby boomers (most are parents today) recognize the endless hard work and sacrifice that their parents made through all the difficult times.

Many remember the best-selling book *The Common Sense Book of Baby and Child Care* by Dr. Benjamin Spock (b 1903), published during the late 1940s. This book was sort of a "how to" for raising the baby boomer generation. But let's face it, there wasn't a book or anything else that could have prepared the WWII generation for raising the boomers. It wasn't easy for either the parents or the children to get through things such as the Kennedy Assassination in (1963), puberty, the sixties generation gap (don't trust anybody over thirty, especially your parents), Watergate, leaving the "nest," and all of the countless other things.

Bibliography

Encyclopedia of American History, New York: Harper Collins, 1996.

Feather, Leonard. *The New Encyclopedia of Jazz.* New York: Bonanza Books, 1960.

Hart, James D. *The Concise Oxford Companion to American Literature.* New York: Oxford University Press, 1986.

Hassen, John. *1997 Sports Almanac.* New York, Boston: Houghton Mifflin, 1996.

Heffner, Richard D. *A Documentary History of the United States.* New York: Penguin Group, 1991.

Johnson, Otto. *1997 Almanac.* New York, Boston: Houghton Mifflin, 1996.

Katz, Ephran. *The Film Encyclopedia.* New York: Harper Perennial, 1994.

The New Grove Dictionary of American Music, edited by H. Wiley Hitchcock and Stanley Sadie, New York: McMillan Press, 1986.

O' Sullivan, Judith *The Great American Comic Strip.* Boston: Bul Finch, 1990.

Rose, Barbara *American Art Since 1900: A Critical History*. New York: Praeger, 1967.

Shapiro, Mitchel E. *Television Network Prime Time Programming,* Jefferson, NC: McFarland & Co., 1989.

Schlesigner Jr., Arthur M. *The Almanac of American History.* Greenwich, CT: Brumpton Books, 1993.

Stich, Sidra *Made in USA: An Americanization in Modern Art*. Berkely: University of California Press, 1987.

Trager, James *The People's Chronology.* New York: Henry Holt Publishing, 1992.

Bibliography

Encyclopedia of American History, New York: Harper Collins, 1996.

Feather, Leonard. *The New Encyclopedia of Jazz.* New York: Bonanza Books, 1960.

Hart, James D. *The Concise Oxford Companion to American Literature*. New York: Oxford University Press, 1986.

Hassen, John. *1997 Sports Almanac.* New York, Boston: Houghton Mifflin, 1996.

Heffner, Richard D. *A Documentary History of the United States*. New York: Penguin Group, 1991.

Johnson, Otto. *1997 Almanac.* New York, Boston: Houghton Mifflin, 1996.

Katz, Ephran. *The Film Encyclopedia.* New York: Harper Perennial, 1994.

The New Grove Dictionary of American Music, edited by H. Wiley Hitchcock and Stanley Sadie, New York: McMillan Press, 1986.

O' Sullivan, Judith *The Great American Comic Strip.* Boston: Bul Finch, 1990.

Rose, Barbara *American Art Since 1900: A Critical History*. New York: Praeger, 1967.

Shapiro, Mitchel E. *Television Network Prime Time Programming,* Jefferson, NC: McFarland & Co., 1989.

Schlesigner Jr., Arthur M. *The Almanac of American History.* Greenwich, CT: Brumpton Books, 1993.

Stich, Sidra *Made in USA: An Americanization in Modern Art.* Berkely: University of California Press, 1987.

Trager, James *The People's Chronology.* New York: Henry Holt Publishing, 1992.

Photo Credits